My First Book about the Alphabet of Freshwater Animals

Amazing Animal Books
Children's Picture Books

By Molly Davidson

Mendon Cottage Books

JD-Biz Publishing

Download Free Books!
http://MendonCottageBooks.com

Read More Amazing Animal Books

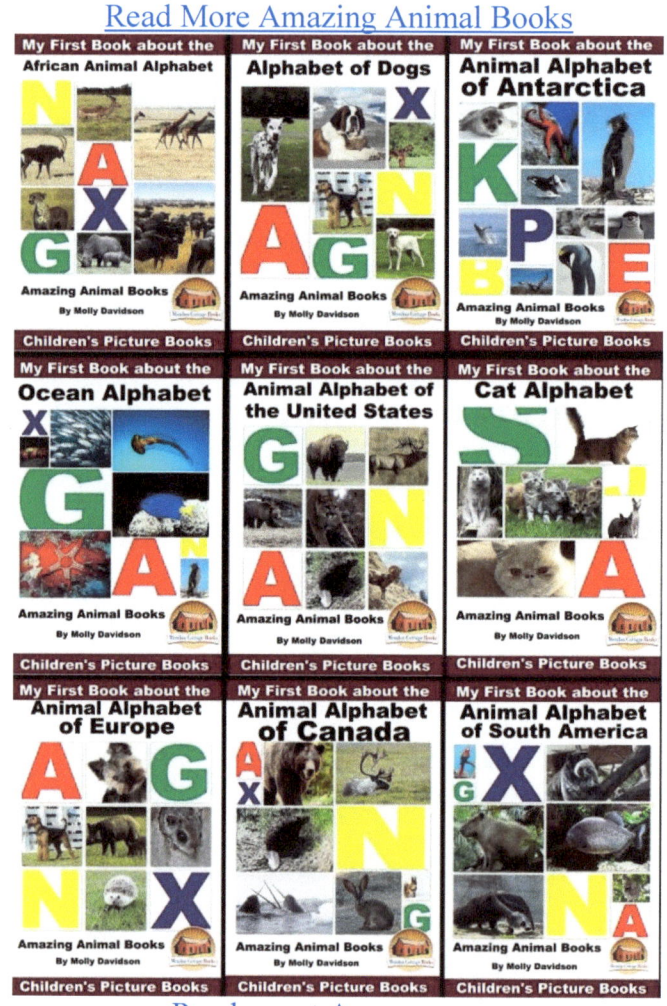

Purchase at Amazon.com

Download Free Books!
http://MendonCottageBooks.com

Introduction

Freshwater lakes and rivers are created as snow melts high in the mountains, and flows down; also, water is collected as rain falls down.

Freshwater provides homes from some animals, and helps others by providing them with water to drink; all species need water in one form or another.

 is for an Alligator.

Alligators can grow to be as long as 18 feet.

If the eggs are kept above 93°F they will be boys, if they are less than 86°F they'll be girls.

 is for a Beaver.

Beavers can swim as young as one week old and can stay underwater for up to 15 minutes.

They use their teeth to cut down trees which they use to make beaver dams, as a protection from predators.

B is also for a Baikal Seal.

Baikal seals are the only freshwater seal; they live in Lake Baikal in Siberia, Russia.

They can stay underwater for up to 70 minutes, if they need to protect themselves or if they are finding food.

C is for a Catfish.

Catfish mostly feed on the bottom of lakes and rivers, and are most active at night, which is called being nocturnal.

Catfish can be anywhere from less than one inch long up to 8 feet.

D is for a Dragonfly.

Dragonflies' eyes are made up of thousands of little eyes that create two larger eyes.

They live around freshwater, not in it, this is where they can find mosquitoes to eat; they also lay their eggs in the water.

D is also for Ducks.

Ducks can be found swimming and eating in lakes, rivers, and oceans throughout the World.

They are very good at swimming due to their webbed feet, and most ducks do not actually "quack."

E is for an Electric Eel.

Electric eels are not actually an eel; they are a species of knifefish.

They have enough electrical charge to stun a human with one shock.

Over 3,000 baby electric eels can hatch from one nest of eggs.

F  is for a Freshwater Dolphin.

Freshwater dolphins are only found in the Amazon River in South America.

They have very small eyes, making it hard for them to see very well, so instead they use echolocation, where sound waves bounce off objects letting them know where food is.

G is the Greater Flamingo.

Greater flamingoes can live in groups, called colonies, of over 200,000 birds.

They eat mostly shrimp and crustaceans which they pick off the bottom of shallow lakes, with their head fully under the water.

 **is for a Hippopotamus.**

Hippos live in rivers, lakes, and mangroves mostly in Africa.

They give birth to their babies underwater, but the baby soon swims to the top to breathe.

Hippos can run faster than humans and are the most dangerous animal in Africa.

I is for an Indian Glassfish.

Quatermass © Wikimedia Commons

An Indian glassfish is also called an x-ray tetra; they are found swimming in South Asia and many fish tanks.

They have a clear body, making it easy to see all their bones and organs.

is for a Jacana.

Jacana birds have super long toes which helps it walk across the water on floating lily pads.

They eat insects and invertebrates that float on the top of the water or that live on the plants in the water.

K  is for a Keelback Snake.

Keelback snakes, also called freshwater snakes, live along creeks and swamps on the Cape York Peninsula in Austarlia.

They are not venomous and eat frogs and reptile eggs.

L is for a Leech.

Leeches are a type of worm, with 32 brains, found in freshwater rivers, marshes, and ponds.

They have suckers on both ends of their body, with three jaws that have sharp teeth which helps them suck blood.

L is also for a Largemouth Bass.

Bass are the most fished for fish in the U.S.

The girls lay the eggs, but the boys are in charge of guarding them until they hatch.

Bass do not have eye lids and their irises do not adjust so it is hard for them to see in the bright sunlight.

 is for a Mute Swan.

Mute swans are one of the heaviest flying birds in the World, weighing up to 26 pounds.

They feed off plants and insects that live in freshwater lakes.

is for a Newt.

Some newts only live in the water while others live in the water and on land, but all are nocturnal, which means active at night.

Many have brightly colored skin, which warns predators that they are toxic and harmful.

 **is for an Otter.**

Otters eat fish, and can dive up to 300 feet in search of food.

They have a tail which is about one foot long; this helps them steer through the water.

Wild otters have a life span of about 10 years.

P is for a Piranha.

Piranhas live in large groups in the rivers of South America.

They have powerful jaws and razor sharp teeth.

They feed on other fish.

P is also for a Platypus.

Stefan Kraft © <u>Wikimedia Commons</u>

Platypuses are the only egg laying mammal and are found in eastern Australia.

The boys have spurs on their back feet which can inject venom causing great pain to humans.

 **is for a Rana.**

Rana frogs lay up to 2,000 eggs in one big sticky bunch that floats on the top of the water.

They live in rivers, lakes, streams, and some neighborhood gardens in Europe.

S is for Salmon.

The name salmon came from a Latin word meaning "to jump."

They migrate upstream to lay their eggs in gravel nests at the top of a stream, after they usually die.

T is for Turtles.

Most freshwater turtles have hard shells.

Turtles have been on the Earth for more than 220 million years.

All turtles lay their eggs in holes that they have dug on land. Once the babies hatch they crawl back into the water.

T is also for Trout.

Trout are a large group of freshwater fish that are related to salmon and char.

One of their favorite foods to eat is flies.

Trout that live in lakes live two or three times longer than those that live in rivers.

W

 is for a Water Strider.

Water striders have long legs that they use to help spread out their weight so that they can walk across the water.

They eat mostly spiders and insects that happen to fall on top of the water.

 **is for Yellow Perch.**

Hadal © Wikimedia Commons

Yellow perch are commonly found swimming in the Great Lakes of North America.

They live in groups, called schools, of 50 - 200 fish.

Z is for a Zebra Danio.

Zebra danio fish live in tropical freshwaters and are popular as an aquarium fish.

They are a small fish growing to be only about 2 1/2 inches long.

It is one of the only fish to have ever traveled into space.

Conclusion

I hope you have enjoyed reading about many of the amazing animals that live in freshwater.

One more fact, fish use their gills to breathe oxygen out of the water, which is why they cannot survive on land.

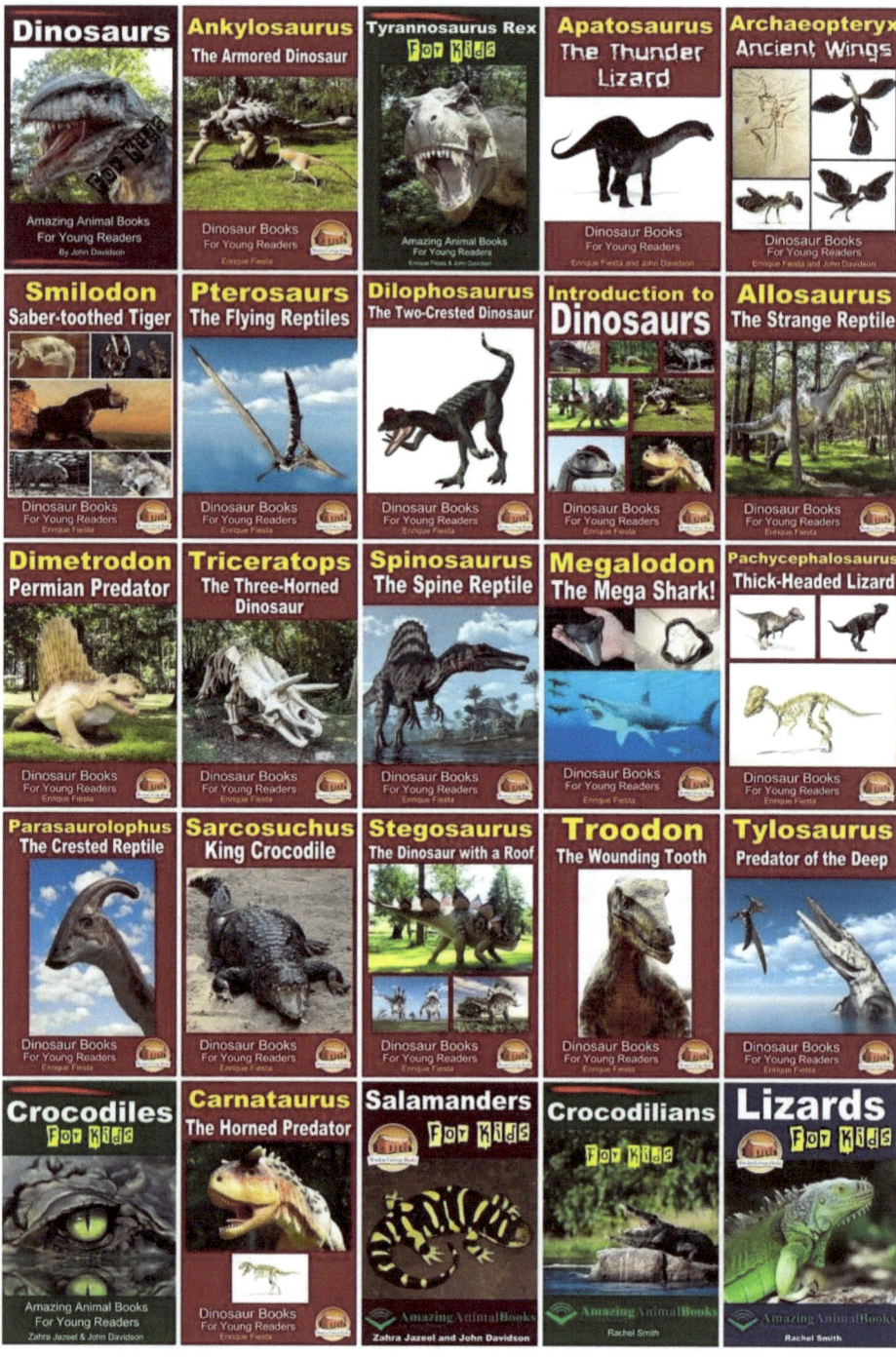

Our books are available at

1. Amazon.com

2. Barnes and Noble

3. Itunes

4. Kobo

5. Smashwords

6. Google Play Books

Download Free Books!
http://MendonCottageBooks.com

Publisher

JD-Biz Corp

P O Box 374

Mendon, Utah 84325

http://www.jd-biz.com/

Mendon Cottage Books
P O Box 374, Mendon Utah 84325